ASSARACUS

A JOURNAL OF GAY POETRY
ISSUE 06

ALEXANDER, ARKANSAS
WWW.SIBLINGRIVALRYPRESS.COM

Assaracus
A Journal of Gay Poetry
Issue 6: April 2012
ISBN: 978-1-937420-16-1
ISSN: 2159-0478
Bryan Borland, Editor
Brent Calderwood, Associate Editor
Philip F. Clark, Art Editor
Copyright © 2012 by Sibling Rivalry Press

Cover Art: "My Black-Haired Adonis" by Seth Ruggles Hiler. Used by Permission.

All rights reserved. No part of this journal may be reproduced or republished without written consent from the publisher, except by reviewers who may quote brief excerpts in connection with a review in a newspaper, magazine, or electronic publication; nor may any part of this journal be reproduced, stored in a retrieval system, or transmitted in any form without written consent of the publisher. However, contributors maintain ownership rights of their individual poems and as such retain all rights to publish and republish their work.

Sibling Rivalry Press, LLC
13913 Magnolia Glen Drive
Alexander, AR 72002

www.siblingrivalrypress.com
info@siblingrivalrypress.com

Assaracus Issue 06

The Poems of Dustin Brookshire
p. 7

The Poems of James Cihlar
p. 19

The Poems of Nicolas Destino
p. 33

The Poems of D. Gilson
p. 44

The Poems of Charles Jensen
p. 56

The Poems of Raymond Luczak
p. 67

The Poems of Glenn Allen Phillips
p. 81

The Poems of Andy Quan
p. 92

The Poems of Jack Veasey
p. 102

The Poems of Jeff Walt
p. 116

The Poems of Desmond Kon Zhicheng-Mingdé
p. 128

A Poem for Ian Young by Gavin Geoffrey Dillard
P. 140

Featuring the Art of Seth Ruggles Hiler
Artist's Biography p. 142

DUSTIN BROOKSHIRE

KISS THIS

DUSTIN BROOKSHIRE is a writer and Dolly fanatic living in Atlanta, Georgia. His work has been published or is forthcoming in *Subtle Tea*, *Ocho*, *Oranges & Sardines*, *Ouroboros*, *Qarrtsiluni*, *Whiskey Island*, *Blue Fifth Review*, *Shape of a Box*, and other publications. His chapbook, *To the One Who Raped Me*, is forthcoming.

www.dustinbrookshire.com

AFTER THE CHANGE*

The blowing of clear wind in your gay hair
makes me realize how you're changing,
and how your hair IS gay—
not gay happy,
but gay I want to sleep with another man.
It was short when we dated,
even after,
but, now, with him,
you're growing it out
because as you said,
He likes my hair longer.
He likes to run his fingers through it
when we're in bed together.
But all I can think about is how gay it looks—
wavy, very nellie, and nellie
is something I've never called you.
It's faggy really.
But it makes me think of change.
How you're changing—
How I'm changing,
trying to find my way out
of this anything but clear wind.

---

*The first line is from Gwendolyn Brooks' "love note II: flags"

WE

Three weeks into the relationship
and it's already:
We love to walk in the park;
we always enter at 10th Street.
We aren't going out that much
because we don't think it fits
what we want in our lives,
and we really hate smelling like smoke.
I tell him Queen Elizabeth
hasn't used the word "we"
in her eighty plus years
as much as he has in the last three weeks.
He says I can't comprehend,
can't connect.
Buddy, I'm no fucking Lego
to connect with a man
just because he's on top of me.

JUST ANOTHER PUSSY POEM

My mother told me it was a bad word,
only saying it starts with "P"
and ends with a "Y" like dirty.
It's a dirty word.
Pussy.
A word I wouldn't use
until I was nineteen.
Never in the context
of I'd eat that pussy
or fuck that pussy.
But, as in,
pussy is power.
And, just because she has a pussy
doesn't mean she gets fucked—
sometimes a pussy does the fucking.
Isn't it true—she who has the pussy
controls a man's world.
I was nineteen when I first said pussy.
saying, "My brother's pussy whipped.
I've never seen anything like it."
He did everything for his girlfriend
as long as she put out.
The lack of calling and visits
cracked my mother's heart.
She said that's what happens
when a guy is serious about a girl—
I mumbled, "Or, pussy whipped."
But this only proves what I'm saying.
Pussy is power.
Pussy can control the world,
and if you haven't figured it out,
I might have a slight case of pussy envy.

BAD FRUIT
for Denise

You're a bad apple, says my aunt.
She's thankful I fell from a different tree.
I won't disagree. Three of her four never
graduated high school. All had shotgun weddings,
and I write letters to one in a Florida prison.
He was on the news—seems like every channel.
I admit: I'm glad we have different last names.
But I'm the apple whose seeds won't bear fruit,
which makes me bad as gay can be.
How does she speak of her son? The hold up.
His pulling the trigger. A bullet to the back of the head.
How does she explain the fruit she bore?
I say it is rotten to the core.

BYPASSING PEACHFORD*

We were driving somewhere to have her repaired.
But, we weren't driving her. She was in the ambulance.
The pills were still in the top drawer of her nightstand.
My sister-in-law the nurse didn't even bother
to check her pulse—no other advice
than 911 when my brother said overdose.
But, I wasn't even in the car. It was my father
and brother. Mother was in the ambulance.
I was in Athens working for the week.
Father didn't call until the next day.
Mother was in the background explaining,
That's not what happened—not that way.

---

*First line is from Denise Duhamel's "David Lemieux"

Dustin Brookshire

THIS POEM WANTS TO BE CENSORED

This poem is on its knees mouthing,
Five dollars censor me long time.

This poem wants to cause a ruckus
like Janet Jackson's pierced nipple—
to give the right wing more than a nipple ring
to sink their communion-taking mouths into.

This poem says bring the black permanent markers
to mark out its lines like school officials
in New Jersey blacked out the yearbook picture
of two male students kissing.

This poem says strike a match
to the page on which it is written
you Hitler-wanna-be mother fucker.
This poem is ready to blaze.

This poem has no problem saying
fuck the Patriot Act. If you think
library records are telling,
then this poem wants to know
if reading Edward Hirsch's *How to Read a Poem*
classifies it as a terrorist.

This poem loves to be dirty but true—
to say getting rid of Bush was needed
because a bush only gets in the way.

Yes. This poem is begging to be censored.
It knows, unlike the ones who will censor it,
censorship will only make the world want it more.

HIV BARBIE
for Denise

Mattel never placed her in circulation.
Barbie doesn't understand why Cuba & Belize
require HIV testing for visitors staying
more than 90 days. Being older
than 15, even though she doesn't look it,
she would have to submit to testing
in Australia. Barbie gripes to Ken:
Who wants to go to Cuba? They only prove
why sanctions are in place. Belize!
Well, what do they have to offer?
And who cares about Sidney
and that damned Skywalk?

Barbie can't comprehend the fuss.
There are no worries of bleeding cuts
or scrapes or sharing needles.
(*Just say no to drugs*, Barbie shrugs.)
Barbie doesn't even have blood
nor openings for necessity or pleasure.
No orifice means none—ask Ken,
the fact often makes him blue.

With her box comes an information sheet
dispelling myths of how HIV is transmitted:
You may safely share a cup with Barbie.
You may safely wipe away her tears.
Meds will not be needed,
which makes Barbie wipe her forehead.
How would she take the pills anyway?

She sits tucked away deep within a Mattel closet.
Infectious Disease Doctor Ken takes care of her,
even though her body will never age,
never be tortured yet temporarily saved by medications,
never having to worry about blood work every three months,
or having to tell friends, family, and fans she's infected.
They'd only want to know how she contracted HIV.

THE FIRST THERAPIST

When I was younger it never bothered me
that guys liked me for my cock—
took me in me their mouths,
the holiest communion.
The way I entered them like the spirit.
I felt holy each time I made a man cum.
Their grunts and groans
brought silence to the haunting voices of the past.
Sex was my first therapy
before I could afford a therapist.
My therapist says my use of sex is unhealthy.
I say, *Big Macs are unhealthy.*
She says, *Sex can kill you.*
I reply, *So can Big Macs.*
She responds, *Dustin, you know what I mean.*
I say, *I'm making a point.*
And, to be even more clear,
let me say this:
I know what I've done.
I know why it was done.
I've been broken. I want to fix me.

MODERN DAY DANCE OF THE SEVEN VEILS
for Jeremy

Would Salome be on YouTube?
Would the video go viral,
spread swiftly like the flu?
Would she dance to Donna Summer,
her hips undulating to "Last Dance?"
Would she destroy the goddamn kingdom
with the power of her hips?

MISSING NAMES

I.

I'm irritated by those people who
overuse the word Christian when using
it to describe themselves—
the same ones who spell Jesus H-A-T-E.

II.

Home from church she's on the phone;
quickly, she moves from praying
for others to talking about them.
Her phone's hot like a whore's bed
on half off day. I wonder
which uses her mouth more,
which one sins more, my aunt or a whore.

III.

He's gay; she's better than that.
Her sin smells sweeter than his.
The Christmas card she mailed was
addressed only to her nephew
leaving off the name of his boyfriend
of six years. The Christmas card he sent
back left off my uncle's name.
She didn't get his statement;
she prayed over that card.

IV.

She's on the phone talking
about her Christmas card ordeal.
Not once does she use the words
gay or, heaven forbid, boyfriend.
That's why she takes so long
to tell her pain, her strife, her story.
She's doing the tango around the issue
even though no one taught her the tango.
It's a sin to dance that close.

V.

Gay.
Boyfriend.
If she can't handle those words
she'd shit a brick if she had to say
the name of the shot I drank last weekend.
Cowboy cocksucker.
Say it auntie.

VI.

She'll pray for him tonight
and for me I'm sure;
she knows my truth but makes
it her own shameful secret,
makes a martyr of herself this way.
I hate to tell her the world already knows,
and the sign on the martyr office reads
Try again later.
I know she prays to a God
who has favorites,
loves some more than others—
he's not the God
I learned about as a child.
While she's on her knees
praying to him,
I want to smile,
walk away, and say—
Kiss this.

JAMES CIHLAR

WHAT MY FAMILY USED

JAMES CIHLAR is the author of the poetry books *Undoing* (Little Pear Press, 2008) and *Rancho Nostalgia* (Dream Horse Press, 2013) and the chapbook *Metaphysical Bailout* (Pudding House Press, 2010). His poems have been published in *American Poetry Review*, *The Awl*, *Cold Mountain Review*, *Mary*, *Rhino*, *Painted Bride Quarterly*, *Emprise Review*, *Verse Daily*, *Washington Square Review*, and *Forklift, Ohio*. His reviews appear in the *Minneapolis Star Tribune*, *Western American Literature*, *Coldfront*, and *Gently Read Literature*. The recipient of a Minnesota State Arts Board Fellowship for Poetry and a Glenna Luschei Award from *Prairie Schooner*, Cihlar is a lecturer at the University of Minnesota in Minneapolis and a visiting professor at Macalester College in St. Paul.

WHAT MY FATHER DID NOT USE

Windsor knot
Recipe

Golden rule
Washcloth

Discernment
Coaster

Benefit
Of the doubt

A dozen
Red roses

Trust
Indulgence

The same bed
As hers

Crystal ball
Repentance

WHAT MY MOTHER USED

Miss Clairol
Custody

Rog & Scotty's
Supervalu

Toni home perm
The Pill

Please Release Me
Pall Malls

The county lines
My father crossed

Jesus, Mary,
And Joseph

Hot water bottle
Irreconcilable differences

Seagram's 7
Rage

WHAT MY STEPMOTHER USED

The color pink
Rotted bananas

Black Galaxy
With fins

Josef's Originals
Lefton wall pocket

Pearl Drops Toothpaste
Herman Miller sunburst

Fridge, oleo
Her son

Paper dress
Trailer in her driveway

My mother's cut glass
And linens

Pot of chili she flung on the wall
Of my mother's apartment

WHAT I DID NOT USE

A day
at work

with my father
Little League

Model cars
Boy Scouts

Paper route
Auto repair

The name
Henry

Tractor
Shoestrings

Braces
Confidence

Driver's License
Playboy

WHAT MY BROTHER USED

White belt buckle
White shoes

Like the ones
Her boss wore

Long hair
To cover jug ear

Tennis racket
Robotron

Friends' houses
When she was drunk

Force
When needed

Shared account
Christmas

Decorations
Mercy

WHAT MY SISTERS USED

Pillowcase
Thumb

Bing
Toy chimpanzee

QT
Lemon juice

Apathy
Mascara

Portable
Turntable

Patchouli
Incense

Midriff tops
Let It Be

Poster of Snoopy
Feelin' Groovy

James Cihlar

WHAT MY OLDEST SISTER AND HER BEST FRIEND USED

Dog turd
In snowball

Lobbed
At her younger brother

Sharp knife
to cut

his Charlie Brown
doll

Gay porn
Shock value

The word
Shit

Lawn chair
Through

The picture
Window

WHAT MY MOTHER HAD NO USE FOR

Rain bonnet
Collapsible cup

Terms
Of Decree

Lampshades
Without cellophane

Eternal
Brown

Burlap
Sofa

Ample
Evidence

Custody
Alimony

Turning
Her back

WHAT MY MOTHER USED LATER

The Rendezvous
Bar

The three B's
Buds

Butts
Booze

Apartment
On Farnum

Long
Distance

Tirades
Medication

Lump
Pressing into esophagus

Hooded sweatshirt
I sent her

James Cihlar

WHAT I USED NOT SO LONG AGO

A poem about plums
My sister

And her husband
Graduate school

Mean streak
A broken glass

Willa Cather
Bicycle

Sun tanning
His grandfather's pajamas

Cooking lessons
Monte Carlo

Broyhill Fountain
Lee's Chicken

His birthday
My fists

WHAT MY EX USED

Promises
A vacant bedroom

Former roommate
Who taught him

Everything he knows
In bed

AIDS test
A single rose

Note in my mailbox
Please move in

His own
Personals

My fear
Of being outed

Green Tupperware
Itemized bill

WHAT I THINK I USE

My mother's
Sixth sense

My sisters'
Toys

My brother's
No nonsense

My father's
Reserve

My mother's
Temper

My sisters'
Shelter

My brother's
Reward

My father's
Escape

WHAT I USE NOW

Victorian
Music stand

Coir floor mat
Rainbow kites

Flying away
Murano glass

Bead bracelet
The Souq

Serigraph
Print

Container
Gardening

The Old Market
Memory

Loss
Prayer

NICOLAS DESTINO

Music Always There

NICOLAS DESTINO is originally from Niagara Falls, lives in New Jersey and works as an English instructor at The College of New Rochelle. His work has appeared in *American Poetry Journal*, *322 Review*, *Bellevue Literary Review*, and several others. He works part-time as a violinist.

SLEEP THERAPY

Things like giraffes, that's all, and catalogue items,
ordinary things; driving in the snow in the repetitive
shapes of snowflakes, and things like fruit markets
and police activity activating the amalgams of scriptures
inscribing all the checklists that qualify a city,
but the real story is the flashing number eight
in a waiting room, outside of which people have held
doors in restaurants for strangers, or have stolen their
cars or parking spaces, or have let doors slam on strangers,
but the real story is that I would give up all
these dirty thoughts for healthcare.

TECHNICOLOR

I once had a million or more friends
from the view on the bridge.
Faceless heads among the colors
of the towers, and the colors of
towers facing the loss of pink to
light blocking sky puffs above
the blocks of faceless heads
that were my millions of friends
from the view on the bridge.

Colors became necessary, a sign
hung on the bridge said so.
When the sky puffs moved
to let back the light, my million friends
turned into colorful balloons
because it was not so simple,
this transformation, heads to balloons,
all floating upward to meet me
on the bridge by the sign that said so.

Nicolas Destino

AMERICAN COOKIES

They were all sleeping at once in the same house

in every permutation of sleeping, and they were neatly organized into their
own beds, like socks in drawers, and every permutation of socks in drawers,
including cotton bolls sleeping in the drawers of the fields, and this was the
house of gentle breathing, especially when visitors said
this is the way it should be, you're doing things right.

They were all proud in their rightness of being right, in right angles under
the red roof of the house, with the right recipe for frosted cookie moons, and
especially the light way they breathed and moved around each other in the
house when another slept.

But the good and right ways of sleeping changed when socks in organized
drawers, and every permutation of order, including recipes for frosted cookie
moons were rearranged, and visitors said
this isn't the way it should be, you're doing things wrong.

They were all sleeping at once in different houses.

LETTER

My dearest Vivaldi, how I miss you, with larks leaving at the right time
opening curtains for the next moment in a set of four.
You ask of my toes, as they begin to numb, something drastic is
on its way—
your internal fire, but for now you're secretly kissing archdukes long ago,
then my toes, but for now these four snowflakes on my fingertip,
evenly spaced in this ordered formation, each a tiny chime of A major
can be rearranged.
See what happens when I move the rightmost snowflake to the left?
The chord is inverted—now I have been dead for centuries
while today you are just being born.

FOR BOYS WITH DELICATE ACHES

For boys who carve their images in water,
always shifting into ripples of faces
then back to water, let there be boys
who will let them be boys outside the image
of boys, no matter what distortions are found
in rippling mirrors, and let them be boys
who will know what their own faces
will look like in armfuls of years into the future,
the simple future with real mirrors.

POEM FOR A HUSBAND

It wasn't known if the ship's men arrived today as heartwrecks, nor was it known if they arrived in love with other men away from ships. When one man held the twitching lobster in the fireball glow of autumn evening, he looked sad, but it wasn't known if he arrived as wrecked, arrived as an ornament in the fireball glow, arrived as a twitching lobster, it wasn't known if he arrived at all.

LIGHT

Without it you're less drawn as my beloved,
    less a painter of cheetahs.
Cheetahs are less themselves
    and more interpretations
        of cheetahs.

SATURDAY MORNING

When you live alone you can put things where you wish. Alone, you can contaminate your own environment and spill olive oil on an orange floating in the sink. You can sink where you want to, in your own particles, part the water in your own sink, create miracles. You can say things like *excuse the mess. Would you like a drink?* When you live alone you are naked more often. If another man is naked with you in bed, you can say *welcome visitor*. If another man contaminates your environment, you can say *thanks for coming over*, and you can clean up after him with old rags only you know where to find.

Nicolas Destino

THOUGHTS FOR SAD TIMES

This winter everything will be better.
The harbingers of music will all be there,
I'll have a new wool suit for the scene
of the buffalo and the owls that will all be

the harbingers of music, always there.
This winter everything will be better—
for the buffalo and the owls and the elk,
and for us in our new wool suits listening

to them, the harbingers of music always there,
perfecting the notes of the songs in the snow.
This winter everything will be better.
We will sit gathered and loved and warm,

with the buffalo and the owls and the elk
perfecting our songs in the snow,
all of us in our new wool suits, listening,
singing, as harbingers of music always there.

FUGUE

Oh, absence of speaking and brittle starfish, and life form
in my bed I cannot name, and feral earth of origins
where can we begin?

Oh, Galileo and his rightness of those
sparkling twinklers, and hangover city of lovers
in loverships and sexual variations

and the life form in my bed I cannot name, and the history
of Beethoven pounding away, and all musical
variations, where can we begin?

And he in my bed I cannot name, in lovership
and his rightness upon me, and something forced,
and myself split in two,

and the suddenness of becoming two things.

D. GILSON

VACANCY LIGHT

D. GILSON, a queer boy from the Ozark Mountains, is a teaching fellow at Chatham University. His chapbook, *Catch & Release*, won the 2011 Robin Becker Prize and is forthcoming from Seven Kitchens Press. His recent writing can be found in *The Los Angeles Review*, *Touchstone*, *Moon City Review*, and *The Rumpus*.

www.dgilson.com

RETROSPECTIVE

When you are nearly a third decade,
look back one. Tell that boy to slow

down, to steal time, to learn Spanish
and not French. Or to learn French

better. To visit France. Tell him brother
never means the things he says, not

faggot, not I promise. Go to Seattle,
live on a houseboat, study anthropology.

Study yourself in the rising tides
of the Puget Sound and soon become

a seal upon a rock washed clear of moss,
but not clean. Clean yourself. Prepare.

Move east. Love a man though you always
thought it'd be a woman. Let the man kick

your stomach, eat it raw. Leave his highway
behind on a yellow bicycle. Eat Doritos,

an entire bag, and make this penance.
Move west again. Or halfway and south.

To Mexico. This is why you should
have learned Spanish in the first place.

HOW I CAME TO PLAY SHORTSTOP

When junking, my mother would say, *have
have a discerning eye, always carry cash,
and never bring your husband.* Every trip
began with a stop for Diet Cokes—I imagined
us as the closest of broads. *Sure*, she would tell
her friends, *I could bring you along, but my son
has a good eye for carnival glass and won't
bitch about his kidney infection the whole
damn time like you, Eleanor.* We'd make
our way through little country towns named
Miller and Crane and Bois D'Arc, my favorite
(*there is something very Parisian here, no?*).
We'd work through flea markets and I,
fascinated and wanting to prove my worth,
pointed to a Kewpie figurine and said *they got
the nostrils right, but that loud rouge is a dead
giveaway for a '30s reproduction.* She seemed
pleased—I was nine and already knew how
to spot the real thing. That night the antique
guides were taken from my room, a baseball
and glove put in their place on the dresser.

AND THIS BIRD YOU CANNOT CHANGE

Today Mama cut Jesus with a box cutter.
It was an accident. The box cutter was dull
'cause I had used it to cut off my jeans.
Jesus ain't our Lord & Savior. She's our dog,
a Wheaton Terrier my brother Lynyrd
got when he sold a whole mess of pills
over in Tallahassee. Lynyrd's in jail now
but I don't mind 'cause I got Jesus to hang
out with. Right now Jesus is mighty pissed
and won't come out from under the porch.
Lynyrd's Christian name is Andrew but
he changed it after his girlfriend, who is
one of Mama's old high school buddies,
told him that when he sings *Freebird*
at karaoke he sounds just like Skynyrd.
And that it makes her wet. I heard all this
because I was outside their bedroom with Jesus.
I giggled and Lynyrd roared outta that room
so fast and told me *Jesus boy! You better get going
if you know what's good for you!* I usually don't
know what is good for me. So then I flew
down to the railroad tracks just past Oak Street
because that's where when I was thirteen
last year I scored some real good crank
and a high school boy let me give him
a BJ behind a rotted out boxcar. But then
he got all pissed because I wasn't very
good at it so he square knocked out
three of my front teeth. The social worker
who comes by the house every other
Thursday asked if Daddy did it and I said
no 'cause I haven't seen him in three
weeks. Then she adjusted her turquoise
cardigan with the lemon yellow stitching
and asked if Lynyrd did it. Again I said
no. She got real quiet and left in a hurry
but said she hoped to see me at church
on Sunday. Jesus nipped at her heels
all the way back to the car. Which is what
he does to Mama too. Which is why she
swung at him with a box cutter today
and why Jesus is pissed under the porch.

DRIVING BACK TO MISSOURI FROM NEW ORLEANS

I force my father to take a detour.
Kentwood, Louisiana, childhood home
of Britney Spears, is only an hour
out of our way. He doesn't want to stop.
He doesn't understand I need to see
this place. Some years later, Dad
will learn his son is gay and fancies
himself some Britney. He does not
understand this fascination. I can't
explain to him what it is to be queer
from the country, to dream in pop
music and choreography, in eye
shadow and excess from the sidelines
of a football game. I think Britney
might understand and though she
doesn't live there anymore, doesn't
come back often, I need to see where
she comes from, to see if life is what
I fear, you can never get away, or what
I dream, you never have to come back.

WHAT TWO MEN SEE

Again we have slinked away
to a cheap hotel in Bentonville,
Arkansas, where I lay wasted
on the sheets. I am alone now.

These sheets are too crisp
and make me think of my father,
who was in the Air Force and
admired such severity in bed

linens, in speech, and in a man.
My father makes me think of
my mother who always told me
not to mess up the sheets and that

making your bed every morning,
first thing, really sets the tone
for your day and I wonder why
I think of them here and now.

You come back into the room
carrying a bucket of chipped
ice and I can see a semen stain
on your boxers. I laugh, wonder

what your wife will think if
she finds it there. You say
*There's a man in the hallway
who looks like a thin, beardless*

Hemingway. This is our night
in Arkansas. At two in the morning,
we kiss, fuck secretly again as scant
vacancy light streams in the window.

D. Gilson

FOR THE SOLDIER IN MEMPHIS SHIPPING OFF
TO IRAQ THE FOLLOWING MORNING

This is the first time I've ever done this
with a man, he says, and what I want
to say is oh honey, do not dismiss
this pretty thing we have, do not haunt
our bed, these sheets or your army-issued
briefs with your wedding band this boiling
afternoon when, like boys, we play house
at the Motel 6. Except one of us clings
to it—the smoke in the curtains, the sweat
that pools in your left clavicle where I dive
in, swear never to do this again, never let
myself love (don't call it love) a man half-alive.
But instead I say *Yes. Now lower. Take your*
time, soldier. Tomorrow will only bring war.

SOMETHING LIKE PRAISE

Praise be to Neruda and his poems,
that tell the beginning, the thousand
ways to say I love you. Praise be
to Plath, the need for fuck you, eat shit
and die you heartless bastard,
her poems the poems I needed when
the man I thought I loved—the one
I gave Neruda to—up and quit
on me. Andy said *the heart's
a violent muscle, opening and closing.*
Yes, I know, and the cliché is lost
in the heart's absolute honesty.
Mostly, praise be to my mother,
whom I call drunk one night,
cry to a time zone away that I will
never love again. She sighs,
says *life is quite a queer thing,
isn't it?* I expect her to hang up,
to say call me when you're sober,
but she cradles the phone in the nape
of her neck as I cradle the phone
in the nape of mine, whispers a story
of when she almost left my father,
but didn't, the story I will retell
myself years later, when broken,
I praise our ability to move forward.

PROPHECY

I.

Phil has Jesus tattooed
on his right forearm
and like this, we are bound,
the formerly faithful youth
of Middle America.
I ask *where did you go
to church camp?*
He smiles, passes
my americano across
the counter. *Ohio.
Southern Baptist. You?*
And I tell him: *Missouri.
Pentecostal.* We laugh.

II.

At the altar near the lake,
I am fourteen and pray
alongside a friend.
He lays hands on me,
says *I know your faith
is weak, but God can
restore it.* Even then,
I knew he would not,
but I prayed in words
I did not know.
My friend, moved
by this coming
of the Spirit, brought
forth his Bible,
leaned in close
to my ear, whispered
what Peter wrote
in the Acts: *it shall come
to pass in the last days.
I will pour out of my Spirit
upon all flesh:
and your sons
and your daughters
shall prophesy,*

*and your young men
shall see visions,
and your old men
shall dream dreams.*

III.

And this was my vision:
Phil at this coffeeshop
in Pittsburgh where
he grinds the beans,
presses them hard
and baptizes them
in scalding water.
When we drink of this,
we call it communion
and become brothers,
sinners washed clean,
however briefly. I see
the thing buried deep
inside of him, inside of me:
the God who is not there.

REVELATION

I gave you a bicycle because the first time
you made me a brown sugar latte I knew
it would be near impossible not to and this
seems irrational now, obsessive, but I dreamt
last night of us by the fire, me the Christ, you
John, the beloved. As I stroked your head,
you sang *Sweet Caroline* in my ear, the smell
of sandalwood on your lips as we began
to kiss, then were engulfed in flame. I awake,
startled to be having this dream again, afraid
of what the soul is trying so hard to reveal.
You will pull espresso all morning and I will
teach, meet you at Starbucks later so we can
ride bikes to the creek, strip there and swim
at a place cool and secret, ours, where no fire
can take us, though I too often wish it would.

RESOLUTION

Even on the east side of Interstate 35
the steam rises from a double americano
this morning—I will stop here more often
for claims of *Progress Coffee will make
you strong just like Paul Bunyan.*
I will. Read a novel a week this year.
One a month. I will read a novel this year
and the landscape is bleak. Outside
the Austin Pipe & Supply Co collapses
so I will find a use for this, salvation
even—I will write it here—immortality
of sheet metal and spray paint, of rust
and hygienic needle. I will give the barista
a good tip and my phone number. I will
give the barista a generous tip, my email.
I will give the barista too-much-of-a tip,
an awkward smile, spilling his drink
all over the counter. I will not disappoint
my mother and I will not drink. I will drink
less. I will not show up to dinner drunk.
I will not show up. *For thou preparest
a table before me in the presence of mine
enemies, thy staff* will beat me upside
the head. You say *get it together dumbass*,
shaking your head. I will maintain.

CHARLES JENSEN

SELECTIONS FROM
NANOPEDIA: THE SMALLEST AMERICAN REFERENCE

CHARLES JENSEN is the author of *The First Risk* (Lethe Press, 2009). His chapbooks include *Living Things*, which won the Frank O'Hara Chapbook Award, *The Strange Case of Maribel Dixon*, and, most recently, *The Nanopedia Quick-Reference Pocket Lexicon of Contemporary American Culture* (2012 MiPOESIAS Chapbook Series). His poems have appeared in *Court Green*, *Columbia Poetry Review*, *Field*, *New England Review*, *Prairie Schooner*, *Willow Springs*, and elsewhere.

www.charles-jensen.com

TRAVEL VOUCHER

I fell into the wave and you laughed, then fell under as well. The ocean's essentially an equalizer that way. On a nearby island, rain fell in a billowy curtain that softened the light against its cliffs. A three-legged dog chased a stick with élan, then joined us in the surf. The sun overhead dimmed subtly for a romantic dinner to which we were not invited. The night came on like a hotel robe we knew we'd give back. On the beach, our feet disappeared into slippers of sand. We wore them like dance shoes. We wore them like fins.

ECONOMIC BAILOUT

When Americans invented money, they had no word for it, so for a while they just called it *you*, like a stranger who comes to town with a bag full of tricks and elixirs. When they rubbed crisp bills against their bodies, they'd say, *You feel like fine-grain sand,* and *You feel like cold rain* when it was coins. Or, when they were poor, they'd tell their friends, *I don't have as much of you as I'd like.* It was a touching statement, and together Americans resolved to end poverty and in the process accidentally created marriage. For a while, no one was poor or lonely because love and money were sharing the same bed and everyone had what they needed. But when they wanted more *you*, they couldn't understand if they needed more love or more money. Over time, all anyone argued about was money or each other. *I've had enough of you,* they'd say, and then some smart person invented divorce.

Charles Jensen

DEFRIENDING

When the man I'd come to love abandoned all hope of his leaky undersea locker getting a key pluck, he sank to me, expelling one long, sad breath. Months of wreckage piled up in his on-again, off-again interest. That weekend, dry, I drop by a party. Across the snack tray, I spy a new man who might be perfect: pre-med, non-smoker, d/d free, doesn't know me. I seal our lips and breathe. Tag-team lungs. Lamprey on host skin like slick velvet crushed flat. My brain, such a rock star, sings, *Is this love that I'm feeling?* In the morning, our lips part like blackout drapes and knives of sunlight slice apart the room. Taking him to his car, preparing to split, we pass by my old Davy Jones in his dark blue suit. Angrily, he could ink the whole room in a huff. How many hearts in an octopus? How many lovers? Ask Cousteau: in the dark ocean, nobody knows.

PARTY FOUL

Outside I felt dance music bass thrum in my chest like anxiety or infatuation or adrenaline, where a moment into the crosswalk my friend vomited like someone pouring from a pitcher of beer. (No.) The night, its threadbare curtain of black above our heads. (No.) A mace, a morning star. (No.) The place where I saw two men kiss: one was a stranger and the other was my boyfriend. (No.) The planets that never appear although we wait. The stars that have already died. (No, no.) Fear as a mantra. (No.) The aftertaste of bile dissolving on the tongue like Ecstasy. A car horn's impatiently curt *toot-toot*. The sheer sky, a dome of diamonds, covering all we won't allow ourselves to see.

HETEROFLEXIBLE

His the first nipple I ever saw pierced in real life. And then I met his girlfriend: sweet, likeable girl with long hair I lovingly named *Bitch*. Eater of all my foods and not enough shame: her voice, singing upper register arias, floating up through air vents as familiar bedroom music. That summer he sauntered the floors all lithe and muscular, carefully shaped but not vulgar. Bitch went away on holiday. I filled his tank with cocktails, yanked him to a bar for dancing. Our bodies, then, touching on purpose. When I lunge for *touché*, the foils of my lips tensile, he decoys. I plunge into nothing, no kissably close connection of our tongues. That summer I was a dope unable to be smoked or patted, not even spanked. We moved along and I forget the rest, but nothing changed. I saw him again, years later, over dinner. I poured the liquor in and waited. He would not budge. Depressed, rejected: I shuffled home and masturbated.

HAPPY HOUR

White rabbit in such a hurry Thursday nights—get to the bar, get fed. Find the tiny door into someone's rumpled bed. That slinky street outside the bar lays down for your weekly march: north bar, south bar, curbside, bus stop. Drag queen star Miss Xena Fauxbia mouths empty promises to the crowd, alluding to your dollar bill's fated future in her g-string. The go-go boy's hips swirl like a planetary orbit constantly coming back to you. White rabbit, his crotch is not a door. Men around you fall like playing cards: red ones, black ones, hearts and diamonds. Your strobed body there, not there. Easily forgetting yourself. White rabbit stumbling drunk or high into the bathroom where the mirror never lies: white rabbit stroking glass around your ears. You dream of passing through a looking glass and vanishing: on the other side, a rabbit hole leads long and deep beneath the streets. This mirror, for you, a mirage.

HIMBO

Me as a masked man, crossing state lines like a lonely felon. Dragging a lame foot behind me: the clever game of the killdeer, who moans loudest when ready to strike. I'm saying I did it: bucked a good pony in the rear just because it rode. Good thing I headed West when I did: Eastern cities dot the night coastline like earrings with white diamond stares. A new man stopped dead in my curly crosshairs. The fickle heart beats two times but sells nothing cheaply. I stroked his hair. I palmed his neck's nape with my murderous hands. The two of us peered up through the moon roof at stars. My beady raccoon eyes, robber baron of bottomless men and their easily ripe lips. Right off the vine. Toward a familiar fog, I walk home alone.

Charles Jensen

CLIFFS NOTES

The beach rolls out ahead of us, soft as Berber carpet. Waves crash in like a series of drunken uncles nobody wants to see again. They throw their foam about like bursts of profanity and beer. Near sunset, we scale the craggy rocks that break the beach in two and, for a little while, observe the human animal in its natural habitat. We see a single fish as we snorkel, skimming the scalloped seafloor, its body so clear we can see right through it. I assure you it's not metaphor and then, when the sun falls behind the island, I memorize your face its thick, honeyed glow.

MANIFEST DESTINY

Ingenuity is a uniquely American virtue. For while Peruvians invented Machu Picchu, this was long ago; Americans have since established Unitarian Universalism, UHF, civil unions, and a series of euphemisms (*underarm*, etc). Antiestablishment types often argue that these new traditions lack utility, but this is untrue. America is the land of opportunity, after all, and where would humans be without America's uncanny knack for ubiquity? We are here; we are there. We invented the Internet. We have Googled you. We invented the camera. Right now, we are watching you.

Charles Jensen

NO VACANCY

On the wall, you see a painting—
something simple like a hay field,
a vase of flowers, a red barn. A
pinprick hole in the canvas lets
light leak through to the next
room, abandoned. And there you
stand, upside-down, removing
your hose from the garter belt. It
sees you. The dark room, the
seedy motel: it's familiar in a way
that unnerves you. You dirty girl.
Money spills from a stiff purse
like poison gas. You dirty girl
smelling of money and gasoline.
The bathroom tile scrapes at your
feet with its gruesome cold. The
water runs. The shower drain
gurgles its death-rattle. The
camera obscura goes dark. The
light seeps into your eyes until not
even the lid can stop it. Not even
a knife. Not even the night.

RAYMOND LUCZAK

ACCUSATIONS

RAYMOND LUCZAK is the author and editor of fourteen books, four of which are full-length poetry collections: *St. Michael's Fall* (Deaf Life Press), *This Way to the Acorns* (Handtype Press), *Mute* (A Midsummer Night's Press), and *Road Work Ahead* (Sibling Rivalry Press). For the LGBT imprint Squares & Rebels, he is currently editing a poetry anthology by gay male writers living in the Upper Midwest for publication in the fall of 2012. He will follow that project with *How to Kill Poetry* (Sibling Rivalry Press) in March 2013. A filmmaker, playwright, and hardcore foodie, Luczak lives in Minneapolis, Minnesota.

www.raymondluczak.com

BOUND AT THE STAKE
after Walt Whitman

These Pilgrims had wanted you burnt at the stake
long before you were born. No one should sex!
Wearing a splash of color was akin to carnal knowledge.
No one wanted their stern ideas of the universe
so they had to find a land where there was no one
with besotted ideas of what the proper religion should be.
Their bones brittled resolve for God's sake.
Laughter and lust would be carefully rationed.
The only wood left burning was made of accusations.

You were the first white American pagan, your chants
committing the joyful sin of blasphemy.
You never sided with any religion. All were equal.
You posed in a slovenly suit from time to time.
You let your hair grow long and scraggly.
Sometimes you left the top of your shirt open.
Such witchcraft of comradeship beat in your chest,
ravens fluttering and shaking loose tired twigs.
I offer you the match. Strike me.

Raymond Luczak

MY FIRST KILL
at Bay Cliff Health Camp, Summer of 1981

    1.

Up close, he was a walking oasis.
I thirsted for that golden-haired man
with his seemingly sculpted pectorals,
shimmering with dribbles of sweat
snaking among the grasses of fur.

He was the first god I'd ever witnessed.
It was as if he'd stepped out of the heavens,
choosing to spend seven weeks
among us heathens who needed lessons
on how to speak, how to adapt
wheelchairs and crutches in a world
far more crooked than us.

Even at fifteen, I knew there was no way
I could pay my just respects to his beauty,
which he'd perfected in the exotic Florida.
Flashes of him erupted in my underwear,
always unbidden late at night.
I never knew such gods could exist *in person*,
and how effortlessly smiles could shatter.

Those nights of ache were so pungent
that I could still see myself lying in wait
in my top bunk in that stuffy cabin,
fidgeting with the patchy stubble
creeping like vines all over chin and throat.
My Adam's apple was now a gnarl
on the trunk of my sapling body.

    2.

She taught me how to pronounce "comfortable."
I always stumbled, never knowing what to do
with that *fort* syllable. How much of an emphasis?
No, the trick was to skip that syllable altogether
so I practiced saying "*comf*-tible" all summer
until I no longer tripped. "Yes, I'm *comf*-tible.
Aren't you feeling *comf*-tible?" "Yes, I am."

Of course, speech lessons were nothing new,
but her photocopies of sign illustrations
were pornographic, exquisitely rendered
far more dirty than my own imagination
where I'd dreamed of signing even though
I didn't know the language. There,
right in front of my own speech therapist
who had studied signs, were all those *sheets*
photocopied and punch-holed into a binder.
She opened to a page and showed me
an artist's rendering of a certain sign,
explicitly so, and with little left to imagination,
usually with arrows thrusting in repetition.
I never knew that was how one should say
"speech" and "love" and "camp" like *that*.
I'd never seen so much foreplay in my life.
Even though they always wore turtlenecks,
they seemed to have no clothes on!

Speech suddenly seemed quaint, old-fashioned.
There was simply no denying the lust inherent
in my hands: I couldn't wait to stroke the contours
of air and space in a thrust of motion.
My hands moaning became louder than firecrackers
exploding in front of my house on Oak Street.
I was shocked that no one reported my disturbances
to the police who'd long monitored my speech,
noting in their records all my ups and downs,
but none bigger than the felony I'd committed
for the sake of my freedom of speech.
I'd become a sign-crazed teenager now obsessed
with the orgasm of achieving signing perfection.

3.

Years before an emotionally disturbed boy
pushed me into the deep end of a swimming pool.
My teacher, eight months pregnant, dove in
after me. I didn't know how to paddle,
chlorine filled my senses, my eyes burned,
found myself clinging to the round basketball
of my teacher paddling her feet.
I don't remember anything after that,
but the chlorine of fear had never stopped lingering.

But that summer in Bay Cliff's brand-new pool
my instructor taught me how to overcome my fear.
I stared at the way lights above bobbed below.
The water never stopped moving. I could see through
to his feet, the dark hairs on his legs undulating,
the looseness of his swim trunks waving along
with his patient hands going, "You can do this."

Once out of the pool, though,
I loved the way he flip-flopped his flat feet
in sandals, as if nothing would ever faze him.
He always grinned at me through his glasses
as if I could read what he was thinking.

He was a solid mass with huge nipples.
He thought nothing of being shirtless
as he guided me, an uncoordinated dolphin
with arms and legs all hopeless fins,
away from the shallow end of the world.
I loved his smile when his hair dripped flat
against his forehead in the split second before
he slid his bangs back. His broad shoulders shone.
I knew he could rescue me, but never in the way
I needed to be saved. He'd never redeem me
if he knew how I secretly longed for him.

He was the one who explained what a faggot was.
He stayed in the Upper Peninsula every summer,
but otherwise he was studying in San Francisco.
He took me aside as his confidante, telling me
how overrun with fags his university was.
He didn't like the city of San Francisco at all
but he needed to earn his degree first.
I was still in awe. He'd been to the Pacific Ocean!
Even pronouncing "California" sounded luxurious.
I couldn't believe that he wanted to be my friend.

Late at night, as the fireflies lured me away
from waving off mosquitoes back to my bunk bed, I knew
no matter how many signs I'd taught him,
he himself would never teach me how to navigate
the choppy waves of desire. Mornings
the god from Florida smiled at me, and I drowned.
I was an unsalvageable wreck with concrete fins.

4.

As the summer wore on, I became less afraid.
It was as if shadows had been brushed away
from the bangs of my hair. I could bask in the sun!
My hands became dandelion whiskers spreading
the seeds of sign among each hearing person
I met. I spoke always with my signs,
not knowing then it was linguistically incorrect,
but never failing to teach a sign whenever I could.
My arms were full of crisp winds that climbed up
the cliffs from the north off Lake Superior
until I felt like an eagle learning to master
the art of staying cool in flight. Watch my wings!

The director of speech therapy at Bay Cliff stood
in front of me. "You shouldn't be signing
so much," she said. "You should focus
more on your speech." She placed her hands
on mine, trying to hush the obscenity of
signs spewing out in front of her face,
but I stopped speaking. "Why aren't you talking?"
I looked down on her hands. "Oh." She let go.
"I'm not goina stop signing—"
When she put her hands on my arms again, I turned
mute. My eyes turned into spears poised to strike.
She dropped her hands and sighed.
With my first kill, I didn't know I'd become a lion,
finally *comf*-tible with the roar of my hands.

RED MAPLE WIFE

My maple hair has caught fire.
I have been sitting too long in this backyard chair,

fallen asleep from the laziness of days gone by.
My hairdresser never told me she'd leave.

I thought my hair would be fully photosynthesized,
thick and fluffy with sparrows darting in and out,

always alerting everyone to my stately beauty,
but no, I find that I've developed too much chlorophyll.

My kingdom of backyard may seem small,
but my follicles are fierce. I respect no propriety

when I spread underground rumors of my invincibility
across borders. Everyone knows my true age,

a lifetime of rings from remarrying Mr. Spring again.
I know how he's seduced everyone in sight.

Worse yet, he knows just how much loneliness costs me.
He doesn't care to understand how much I've primped

and saved so much of my blood for him. From this chair,
I see him still flirting with pretty young saplings,

whispering promises of marrying them once he divorces
me, this gargantuan bitch with prickly jowls.

I don't understand how he could so easily forget
how these anorexic babes, full of puffy dreams,

never survive the first bitch-slap of snow. They will
wither. He always leaves them once he remembers

what a tough bitch I am when friends abandon him.
I always have a field day in divorce court.

Now homeless, he begs to sleep with me.
I know he'll leave me again, but he's so damn beautiful.

CALENDAR CENTERFOLD

The teacher hates me, but boys and girls love
the checkerboard style of my numbered skirts.
No one cares what top I'm wearing that month.
They check my grid when they come in the room,
and stare at me when the teacher looks down.

I am their first schoolyard crush. I promise
gift-filled Christmas breaks, Easterly respites,
languorously hot summer vacations,
and rapid-fire weekends free of homework.
I dare blush, the lucky recipient
of their stolen glances. I count their dreams.

I am their first kiss of mortality.
One day they will grow up and find me gone.
The schoolyard's no longer the world it was.

LIBRARY SHELVES

My eyes knew how to worship books:
the jaggedness of lines criss-crossing,
the juxtaposition of circles paired,
the jangling of words stringed together.
They leap, luminous laser lines
darting down the upstream of my purple rods
straddling each optic nerve deep into
the waterfalls of my brain. I close eyes
to frolic with each sensation, a dream
singular into itself. My mind is a gallery
of photographs indexed as only a child can,
and only in a way a man can remember
without pulling open a musty drawer
of index cards revealing Dewey numbers.
The metal rods holding these call cards
have crumbled into powder, into red gold.
The dust of childhood is on my fingertips.

THE RICHNESS OF SPIT
after William Shakespeare

1.

It was the golden age of cross-dressing. Women weren't allowed to act onstage, so actors dressed up in dresses, shawls, and frilly gloves. Everyone in the audience knew this, so it was always good for a laugh, especially when a man wore a different dress the next time he returned.

2.

From behind the curtain William Shakespeare watches the actor Richard Burbage go through his motions on the creaky pull-stage. How that man could easily make everyone chuckle and laugh with a single bat of his eye!

3.

The iambic pentameter controls speech much like indentations of land with water where it should go. Rhyme no longer has reason to irrigate.

4.

No record exists of whether Mr. Shakespeare ever wore a dress onstage and gave a chaste kiss to Mr. Burbage. Speculation is what drives audiences to come see the truth for themselves. What's laughable is their gullibility: what truly matters is not what happens onstage but behind closed doors. For all we know, Mr. Shakespeare decoyed all.

5.

In those days no one was a director. Memorizing, memorizing. Ah, the lines! That darn snake-snarl of words again. Actors spoke the language of those who flocked to their shows. How strange and repulsive our modern English, remade in that television-standardized accent, would sound to their ears!

They would stand there, disbelieving that we of highfalutin education could render their memories into illegibility in the name of authenticity. No richness of spit, no bump-that-elbow chuckle at the undercurrent of pun, no acknowledgment of the bawdy filth the actors spoke backstage. All that memorizing for not even a slap-your-thigh gut belly laugh?

6.

He listened without judgment. That was *the* secret to his writing. His ears told him all he needed to tell his actors what to say. That, and the constant reading of precious books helped.

7.

Scholars world over would die to see the original copy of the plays he wrote. Copies in his own hand do not exist. No such thing as mimeograph or photocopy in those days. Memory and repetition were the only job security for these actors. Speak, time your entrances well, or die!

Rumors of faking his talent in these 37 plays still persist. Hesitations and debates thrive in such a cottage industry. Queen Elizabeth and James I are no longer around to order executions on the sly, so all's fair in love and war.

Mud is constantly slung in these ivory-white towers, so much that these splotches of mole-brown wet on the wall become considered as "art" and "valid statements" if only to avoid the unseemly task of cleaning these walls. The honesty of whiteness becomes a critical derision.

8.

He lay there not thinking of his wife Anne or the children he'd sired with her but the fair youth for whom he'd poured himself into these strict fourteen lines with tenderness and ache. Words and meaning rolled around like a ship amidst an angry sea of want on his tongue. No, he would never tell a single soul his name nor tell the fair youth for he couldn't read anyway. It would be centuries before a cheeky fellow named Oscar Wilde decoded his secret.

9.

When he was young, ale was all he had some nights in the pub. Small talk was mere appetizers to a meal that he couldn't afford. The crackle of fire lulled him into sleep. Sometimes if he stayed close enough, it would be loud enough to mask the roar of hunger.

He shut the spoiled child's needling of his stomach and opened up the mouth of his brain, playing around with entire lines before he set them forth on paper. Never enough paper; they were expensive. Ink and quills too. Careful, careful, he always had to be.

No one thought about calories or the amount of fat sizzling there in a cast iron kettle. Just ate whatever possible. Never knew sometimes where their next meal came from.

10.

Sometimes the writing got tiring. Who cared about what Hamlet thought? Or that silly-head Juliet?

Writing the history plays were the hardest, trying to kiss the royal ass. The only way he could endure those mind-numbing stories was to play with the language, make it sing a bit more than before. Sometimes he rewrote lines to affect the rhythms of folk songs he'd heard out on the road. Ah, music!

Anyone who could play a music instrument was a rich man in poor people's eyes. How sweet it was to hear something orderly yet emotional after a day of dung and sod. Music was the key to all their dreams. All they had to do was to clap and sing when the fiddler strummed away.

11.

Everyone wanted to be next to Mr. Burbage once the show was over. It didn't matter if they had to strike the set, roll things up, and stuff it onto the lanky cart for the next leg of their tour. Mr. Burbage was always full of high spirits once ale entered his blood. Memories of mimicking people he knew while growing up came to the fore once he saw he had a ready-made audience. Laughs bounced off the beams and walls. He never noticed Mr. Shakespeare staring intently at him from a dark corner, not knowing how much Mr. Shakespeare wanted that gift of charisma and mimicry.

12.

Walking the long and ponderous road from one town to another, the actors memorized their lines, often improving on their rhythms. Their sole copy of these plays transcribed by hand was their most precious hymnbook.

The first time Mr. Shakespeare heard them butcher his lines when they returned to the Globe, he was furious. But once the fury faded away like embers of a campfire, he listened as if he'd never heard them before. By God, they had improved on his writing. They made him sound better!

It was all about the bloody ear.

13.

Late at night Mr. Shakespeare's bones in his crypt still rattle, no blood left in the marrow. Footsteps after centuries of wonder and worship are like injections of blood. No one cares about Mr. Burbage or Ms. Hathaway or any of the people who acted with him onstage anymore. He knows history's lost all track of him except these new and improved lines. Just a name now loaded with meaning in the death of classrooms.

Back then his name meant that he was a shrewd businessman who happened to write what audiences wanted to hear. He was envied for all that money! He no longer cared about the art. He was too tired, more interested in earning even more now that Mr. Burbage was gone, a legend among those who knew him. No one cared about Mr. Shakespeare as a person; he was actually quite boring, his creative ambition dried out of him. He was all money and land now.

If alive, Mr. Shakespeare would roll his eyes and shake his head at the numerous fictions and legends concocted out of the few incontestable facts about his life. Including my own lame attempt to re-imagine him as something that he probably never was.

He'd cock his head and peer into my eyes. I wouldn't be able to understand his accent thick with the dust of centuries. But from poet to poet, I would sense what he'd say should he master today's bewildering English: "Rubbish. No music your poetry are. At all!"

14.

Everybody used to want to be the next Shakespeare, but no, all the fair youths want to be the next hot filmmaker. It's all about the connections, the deals, the distribution, the constant media saturation, the buzz.

Romance, an artificial device reconstructed to fill more theater seats, is now a middle-fingered sonnet.

BOWL OF STONES

"He's dead now." The earthen bowl brims with stones
all bleached with no trace of elegy left.

Water, poured in, seeks equilibrium
between stone and air, firmly in control.

The rim cups my dead eyes in a mirror.
My breaths long to ripple across your face.

Rise up and break the surface, I implore.
You still shimmy, a dolphin playing games.

Storms brew around my face as I try smiles,
an art overdone from your funeral.

In the distance I hear your call to swim.
My fingertips skip stones inside the bowl.

The waves haunt me with promises of sand
hotter than coals, forgiving as sugar.

GLENN ALLEN PHILLIPS

SIN CITY MASS

GLENN ALLEN PHILLIPS teaches both mathematics and English at a Texas community college while finishing up his Ph.D. His poetry has recently been published in *The Alembic*, *Compass Rose*, and *RFD*. In addition to writing, Glenn enjoys traveling, swimming, and helping people simplify—mathematically and otherwise.

PATIENCE

Should I buy heaven
with this half-dead heart?
Bleeding no more than
I am loving, a four-
chambered scab cowering
behind my maple ribs?

Should I tie up my
genitals with prayer string
and wait for them to bloat
and blue and break off
like Greece at the
hands of the Papacy?

Should I hunt my brothers
down and nail them to Wyoming
wood, burn them in faggots on
the leather-clad streets of Castro?

Should I fuck the heavenly hips
of hetero-normative America,
loving her even less than
she loves me?

Or should I just wait for
the last days, when the sun
and the Son have both burnt out,
when I take your hand in mine,
put my cheek to your rough chin
and tell you what this purchased
congregation never thought we'd hear.

IF
for Josh in San Francisco

If I ever became famous
beyond university and
coffee shop circles,

if my poetry ever becomes
mandatory reading for
college freshman and
literacy programs,

if I ever give a national address
at inaugurative steps, with this beard
and heavy southern tongue,

if I am ever assured
that my poetry, with
its origami wings,
will find you,

I will publish this poem,
drop it like confetti over your
parade of a city and help you
breadcrumb your way back to me.

Glenn Allen Phillips

ON SHARING THE L-TRAIN WITH AN ITALIAN BALLET DANCER

The young man across from
me is wearing makeup,
nothing too dramatic, a little
concealer, a light layer of base,
gloss but no lipstick, and
just a touch of mocha to
darken his perpetually arced brows.

His blue and brown street shoes
are in second position with
impressive turn-out considering
how he is sitting.

His fingers are long and laced
and, I believe, would have
thrown a soccer ball or plucked
lemons from trees in another life.

His pinned hair is almost regal.
His scarf severs his head
like a Roman bust.

As he stands for his stop,
he moves into third position.

I half-expect to hear
a staccato string piece
as he *picque* turns to
the piss-covered doors.

BLOOD TESTS

I'm scared I'll die here
in this little matchbox
of a waiting room.

The brown chairs
and immunization fliers
are a sterile comfort
that fills up my stomach.

The ghosts are impatient
and pace in small circles
about the magazine rack.

They brush open year-
old issues of *Sports Illustrated*,
revealing waxy photos
of healthy bodies.

The fluorescent lights
flicker in their wake,
the room shudders
like empty clothes, hung
on a sun-less day.

PARIS

I want you in Paris
on lamp-lit benches
on cobble-stone streets
on golden bridges
on cathedral glass
on moveable graves
on wine
on bread
on *croques St. Jacques*
on *rue de Rivoli*
on German tourists' backs
on gypsy beds
on fruit stands
on Monets and Da Vincis
on carrousels
on Pei's translucent pyramid
on the steps of Sacre Couer
on Napoleon's tomb
on our little island, straddling the Seine.

I want you in Paris
hands sewn at the wrist
finally peaceful in this long field of war.

HOMOSEXUALITY

How casually you hold the word
in the cup of your tongue

the weight of an asp
the echo of an oven
the taste of a pin
the feeling of the building

just before it leaves your feet.

EXONERATED

My father, an unwitting imitation
of my grandfather, was absent
during those formative years
when boys learn about girls
and fast-pitch baseball and
how to hold a loaded gun.

So, I, being ignorant and empty,
grew up learning about music,
how to vie for attention, and
the subtle differences between
a girl and a loaded gun.

It wasn't until I first tried to
shoot either that I realized
I was not my father.

And it was not him, the stars,
or my rocky adolescence that made me
his antithesis. It was luck, pure luck,
that made me put on the same shoes
and run the other way.

SEX

This orchid fire,
this cotton candy obelisk,
this Merovingian apple,
this comet
this dead horse
that swells in my gut
         like a wave that will not break.

THE FIRST POEM

How many poems have I written
with a substituted she, parading pronouns
which protect me from stones, nooses,
and empty tables?

Would that I could rewrite the first one.
Not more than thirteen, I would claim
that his eyes are blue like my mother's
and vacant like a mountain town
just after the snow.

A TOAST

For misery and open roads,
I'll raise my glass.
For sex and silhouettes
and wind between your toes,
for the well-spoken and the damned
and the waxy fruit that perches
in the foyers of both, I raise my glass.

I'll raise my glass to the poor
and the unyielding, the bleeding
mothers and the fags tied around
this country like blue-eyed ornaments.
To the Homecoming Queens and
their dissolving kingdoms, to cigars,
cigarettes, and crack-pipe crucifixions,
I raise my glass.

To you and your skeletons,
to me and mine,
to us and ours,
I raise my glass,

a sacrament at this sin city mass.

ANDY QUAN

NAKED SKY

ANDY QUAN was born in 1969 in Vancouver, a third-generation Chinese-Canadian and fifth-generation Chinese-American with roots in the villages of Canton. He is the author of four books. His first collections of poetry, *Slant*, and short fiction, *Calendar Boy*, were released in North America in 2001. *Calendar Boy* was published in Australia by Penguin in 2002 and was nominated for a Lambda Literary Award. In 2005, *Six Positions: Sex Writing by Andy Quan* was published by Green Candy Press and in a special hardcover edition by Insight Out Books. Quan was recognized in 2005 as Writer of the Year by both the Charity Erotic Awards and the Sydney Gay and Lesbian Business Association. In 2007, his second collection of poetry, *Bowling Pin Fire*, was published through Signature Editions of Winnipeg, Canada. His fiction, poetry, erotica, sex writing, and essays have appeared in over sixty anthologies, literary journals and magazines in North America, Australia, Spain and the United Kingdom. After living in Toronto, London, and Brussels, Andy has lived in Sydney, Australia since 1999.

www.andyquan.com

NOVEMBER, START OF SUMMER

i.

Thirty-eight degrees. Windless. Worse on the asphalt.
Any hotter and rails would have buckled. Trains ran
slow that day. If I start with the weather, it's to pretend
it's not always with myself. Though here's my complaint:
unlike nimble Jack, I fell on the candlestick, it not only
penetrated me, but the wick is growing, twisting up
around my spine through my ribs looking for escape.
So I went to one of those dark places that most gay men
don't tell their straight friends about, pounded the maze's
corridors and forgot the sun outside. Sisyphus trod
up and down; our punishment is circular, chasing one
another's tails. At last, someone turned around. He had
the most un-gay hair I'd ever seen. Poofs are coiffed
with product, or shaved short, but his thick ruddy
coils high on his scalp, almost hid the rest of him.
I couldn't coax him into a cubicle. He'd been inside
for hours and was spent. But I sank my hand into
those burnt red cords and pulled him like an anchor
to my mouth, and we kissed, clanging against
the lockers and groping each other. The wick emerged
from my right ear and was lit by his crimson hair.

ii.

The next day I felt lifted and light
and forced to notice I was something
called happy, which made me realize
I hadn't been the whole month before.
I'd thought what I needed was some
rumpy-pumpy, hip-swinging action
to stop me thinking. But sex mixed
with desperation or compromise
can make things worse. A kiss was
enough. On my cycle home from work
I saw strings of shoes laced together
and thrown over telephone wires, a man
playing soccer with his mutt, two men
in the middle of a sidewalk trying to
put socks on a girl. A spent jacaranda
flower fell from a high branch. I rode
towards it, let it hit me in the face.

DOWN TO YOU

I trampled those days, a lion, believed
in myself with a ferocity that has since
never been the same. They were days
when self-knowing became real, a dented
bud of a tulip infused with its own
fragility and what it might reveal.
I'd discovered *Great Men*. This late
in the century, in so vast a country, so
few gay poets. On my invitation, you
read for the university's first gay
pride week. The dance that night,
dining tables upended, chairs stacked
in corners, nervous men and women
from town mixed with students. I dressed
in what I hoped gay men might wear. You
asked my straight friend to dance, he tried
not to show how proud he was not to
be an oaf, and when it was our turn, after
odd late-eighties tracks and disco throw-
backs: *everything you held high and told
yourself was true*. It was my first dance
with another man, my right hand
awkward upon your hip. You told me
it was your favourite Joni Mitchell song.
We glided, slow-motion skaters, on that
cafeteria's hardwood floor, the man I
would become blooming in the distance,
pairs of men and pairs of women in our
orbit, dim lights suspended from the old
rafters above. *As the days come down to you.*

A HALF

A first for everything: the touch
down on the old island, the tube
ride to the hostel, though two
kind blokes offered a mattress,
pointed me to FF. I wasn't drawn
to the shaved heads of pale
Londoners but to an imposter
Englishman, an American football
jersey across his wide shoulders.
You've never tried it, mate?
You really should.
But he was careful, this devil gave
me only a half. *Your first time.*
Pressed it into my hand.
What I wonder now:
what if it had worked?
As when I discovered a taste
for fine food and never looked
back. I was twenty-two, open
to the world, I felt
as if I had sculled a tall
flute of champagne and though
I did try to kiss that faux
athlete, something
would tell me later my first
ecstasy hadn't worked.

Andy Quan

QUIET AND ODD

Darren Lee and I were superstars, unafraid to swing
from the highest branch of his backyard's gnarled
apple tree, we terrorized insects, older
high-school kids, made snarky remarks about
Mrs. Kopinski in the corner house simply because
we could. We sang: *Jesus Christ /*
Superstar / Who in the hell do you think you are.

"What a shame," adults told us. We couldn't speak
our ancestral language. Nor could our mothers! Tell
them they've lost *their* heritage. What's the use anyway
of those clattery loud towers of nine tones, building
blocks flung at you in too bright colours?

Besides, we were not Bennett Ho whose mother
banned him from sex education class, not Adrian
Tong with his rice-bowl haircut (the fringe swinging
round his head like a carousel of animals). Brian Tom
not yet into his teens expected only bad things in life
so as never to be disappointed. Not Jacob Chiu
whose Mom shaved his skull, everyone wanted to
feel its tiny combs against their fingers. Dominic
Kong was certainly not us, he told people he didn't
know Chinese but who could follow his broken
English? Definitely not Joseph Fong who stepped
in dog poop and didn't care, the playground
suddenly the Titanic sinking, passengers wailed
ABANDON SHIP!
          It wasn't just that they were odd.
They were quiet boys. Not like us, nails on chalk
boards, fire drill alarms: when my voice broke
I couldn't even whisper without getting in trouble.
We reckoned their tongues got caught on the way
out of their mouths like jackets on doorknobs
as they rushed outside, their mothers calling them
back to do their homework, mind their grandmothers,
though even they'd pretend they couldn't hear
or understand whatever language shouted after them.

Andy Quan

LETTERS BACKWARDS IN TIME

I. *never kissed*

you're seventeen, never kissed a boy
but in a few years, it'll land on you
like a sloppy whale
mistaking shore for sea

you'll swim past the undertow
to caves and rock formations
from your first waking dreams
and others you haven't had yet

you'll know the insides of mouths
the clam's lush pink secrets
how to   conserve breath
            cast nets
            dive without panic
how to read the ocean's salt skin
your ears underwater
flesh and cartilage humming to sleep
the school of dancing minnows
in your ribcage

you will see through eyes
that know humility:
            mermen rising
            your heart's wayward shapes
            worlds around you, above and below

II. *trying on clothes*

so much naked sky in your eyes
one of those endless prairie canvasses
though you've yet to see one

I'd say *relax, slow down, easy*
but there's such beauty in that
alchemy of optimism and innocence

each day a Shakespearean drama
comedy even, days condensed into
contained acts, grand themes

Andy Quan

a savvy and overconfident voice
your body trying to catch up
still testing out walking, laughing

gestures that years later will
announce you instantaneously
are only just new blooms

I won't tell you now: the world
is not as important as you know it
the wounds will be such soft scars

time will smooth out, perhaps you'll
forget some years how old you are
accidentally lose names and faces

maybe even these faces around you
tattooed into your sight
all so impatient for the world to begin

SINKING

It's not supposed to be over
the showy languor of summer
the slow arithmetic

of a sun-addled brain.
Now the sky disassembles
our chance to panic

at dropping temperatures, leaves,
washed away in grey torrents.
All week the pavement, air,

buildings dissolve
into each others' casings
yet only two weeks past in

a balmy Austrian August
the leafy bounty
in his mother's yard

Peter gathering flowers
with Kurt
laughter afterwards

the spilt water, damp carpet,
the long stems too heavy
for the shallow vase

Peter rested on the couch
bloated from combo-therapy
the wild effort to drown

the virus in many ways.
He died two days later.
I worry about Kurt

the flashbulb change of seasons
now he's been widowed twice.
the yard is flooded

the order of grass
replaced by water
the ground underfoot

gives way beneath the dense
weight of hyacinths.

Andy Quan

THE LEG CROSSER

A man's right-angled knee
is what money is made of
the outer bump of the ankle
rested across the other leg
and just behind the knee
a wide triangular space
for the testicles to breathe.

A lady's pose would suffocate
the thighs engulfing each other
so bold the forward knee
so wanton the free-kicking foot
you could tip out of balance
with such missing solidity.

> *What happened was prophecy*
> *I tipped over*
> *out of my own masculinity*
> *into schoolgirl crushes on other boys.*
>
> *I also crossed my arms incorrectly*
> *like shivering instead of defence*
> *crossed myself profanely in church*
> *and my eyes, when crossed,*
> *frightened rather than amused.*
>
> *When I crossed my delicate fingers*
> *long and toothy and curved like crescent moons*
> *I wished for the unimaginable.*

Andy Quan

SETTING

Venus. Dusk. I've never witnessed this effect: pinhole through
cobalt blue, startlingly white, edges sharp. I stare at it as if in
a contest not to blink; she starts to travel slowly as if man-made
slides back into place. My opthamologist lover tells me: *If an object
of focus is sufficiently bright, the pigment in your retina's cone-shaped
photoreceptors will bleach out and cannot regenerate until you look away.*

But Venus isn't fading, she's moving and now disappears behind
cover. Cloud cliché rings in my ears: wisp and billowing tapestry,
heavy thunderheads. Most of the sunset is hidden but far off to
the west, a window appears, original, striped with thin horizontal
lines lit in gold and pink, a portal. Between us and the shore
the sand is pock-marked with tunnels: emerging from mounded exits

crabs of a type I've never seen, vaudevillian, pairs of eyes high
on vertical stalks, quotation marks, their thin legs shuffle like the keys
of an old-fashioned typewriter, fill in sentences between. The crab's
torso floats forward, tiny office chairs on wheels. I'm struck they look like
cartoon or illustration when, in fact, it is the other way around. Reverse
translation not unlike these photos. The camera captures faces,

emotions, lies, miniature details that create time and place. But not
this, grand next to small, not even large alone: clouds, horizon.
My camera's setting for "dusk" saturates sky into reds and pinks.
On "normal", it's just light and dark, no occasion at all. When filtered
it is not what we witness but closer to how we experience a *sunset*.

I stare at you without blinking as if you'll fade or duck out of view.
It's not lack of trust, just leftover disbelief — that all of this is true:
fluffy white..., island, planet, crabs. The pressure between our shoulders
leaning into each other, the six muscles in our eyes that allow us
sight in all directions and Venus reappearing, on high, above us.

JACK VEASEY

THE AGE I WAS

JACK VEASEY, a Pushcart-nominated poet, is a Philadelphia native who has been living in Hummelstown, Pennsylvania, for over 20 years. He is the author of ten published collections of poetry, most recently *The Sonnets* and *5-7-5* (both from Small Hours Press, 2007).

MR. MARTIN

Mr. Martin was my high school typing teacher
At an all-boy Catholic school.
He was also the first man I ever loved.

Right after last period,
I'd stop by to see him before I left school.
It never occurred to me
That anybody else
Might think this strange.
I'd babble about nothing
While he wiped the writing
Off the chalk board, banged erasers,
Put the plastic cover
Over each machine.

I never wondered
What he thought of
My devotion. Everyone I knew,
My family included,
Treated me as if
The notion that I might have any feelings
Were unthinkable. I just expected him
To do the same. I never imagined
The pangs I felt
Showed in my eyes.

He wasn't a big man.
His cheeks turned bluish
In the afternoon
From stubble whose replenishment
Impressed me. He wore his short black hair
Slicked down, smelled like
A cigarette, rolled back
His white shirt sleeves.
He'd often stand
And watch his students pound away
With forearms crossed
Over his chest. I never thought
He saw me watching him.
When he'd bark
Instructions at us,
It would always strike me

Jack Veasey

That he sounded like
A gangster on TV.

Of course, the other kids in class
Raised the first questions
In the cruelest way they could.
One asked him to say
That he would see me later
In the locker room,
And, thick head that he was,
He did, in front of all of them.
I felt as though
He'd slapped me. He could tell
Something was wrong,
But it took him awhile
To figure out exactly what.

When he got married,
I went through several reactions,
And they puzzled even me.
I could discuss them
With no one.
I felt like I was losing
My connection with him,
Though I'd still see him
Each day. I was hurt
He didn't ask me to the wedding.
I wished I could show him
I was happy for him, though
That wasn't quite the truth.
I felt like I should give him a present,
Though, thank God, I didn't.

I had a girlfriend, too,
Though mine was a "beard," as they say,
That I was using
To delude myself.
When she (wisely) broke it off with me,
I panicked. I even swore out loud
In front of Mr. Martin.
He objected to
My language—he'd already
Started distancing himself—
And told me not
To come to see him anymore.

Jack Veasey

I stayed home from school
The next day, claiming
That I was sick.
I was amazed
When the phone rang,
And it was him.

He asked why I wasn't in school.
I repeated my lie.
He said, with anger,
"What about tomorrow,
And the next day,
And the next?"
I heard myself blurt out,
"I didn't think you'd care"
And then he answered,
"Well, I do."

I went back to school
The next day—though, from then on,
I'd only visit him
On rare occasions.
When our eyes met,
It was awkward.

I began to live my life
Outside of school—outside
Even my dreams.
I began to do things
I'd denied I even
Thought about.
I learned that love can hurt you
Even worse
When it's expressed, even
Returned. Eventually, I left
High school
And home.

As for Mr. Martin,
I have no idea
If he's still alive,
Although he gave me
My first evidence
That I was.

Jack Veasey

AN INEVITABLE INSIGHT
For my 30th birthday. 4/4/1985

I saw Ron tonight on the subway—
First time in nine years.
With him were his strapping teenage sons.
They were laughing, heading
For some ballgame, for some place
Where I would not know who to root for
(being not preoccupied enough
With power politics, and also
Too distracted by male beauty).

Both sons are beautiful
Now that they look like their father.

I remember the canoe trip
With the four of us, when Ron and I
Were lovers, shortly after his divorce
And not so long before our break-up,
When we drifted off on different trips
And joined each other's missing person's lists—
I in his past mind, he in mine.

But, back then, both sons
Had accepted me, their father's "funny" friend,
A scrawny kid
Whose hands had always talked too much,
Whose hair hung down below round shoulders,
So unlike their father's shoulders,
So bereft of
Heft and brawn.
They had ignored
The obvious, and let the love go
Where it went, not knowing
It would one day go away.
But anyway, we'd shared a lot that day,

So I was tempted
To call out, wave, make
Eye contact, penetrate
Their heady jargon of fond slaps
And gentle jostles.
But I brought myself
To do none of these things,

Really not sure
They'd recognize me,

Because those boys
Are now the age I was
When Ron was more than memory to me,
When I was young enough
To feel young love
And love it. I let my lover go,
And I grew older,
But I never thought
They would; all things
Are as we left them in our minds
Until time tells us otherwise.
And so they got off, laughing,
At my stop, not having seen me,
And I didn't. I was simply
Dazed, too much to move,
Caught clinging
On another kind of ride,
Too stunned to stand up
For another stop or two,
Not nearly ready to remember
So much difference
And distance, or
To feel a sadness I had said
Was dead, or to see those young men
I'd believed still children,
Or to wonder whether
They remember me,

Now that I see
My life, illuminated
But unmoving, like a station
Standing still and
Shrinking steadily,
Receding
Through a dingy window
As the distance
Lengthens, left behind
The surging, roaring, blurred,
Relentless forward rush of
This
Grey
Train.

ADVERTISING FOR LOVE

The model's projecting himself
Through the camera lens—he's
The photographer, too—
Like Narcissus, but he can't
Fall through. He smiles
With blinding perfect teeth,
Bats long-lashed eyes
Clear as a lake
No one's allowed
To swim in.
But I'd bet some
Have drowned there.

Jack Veasey

AFTER THE LAST MORNING AFTER
1984

Eddie's dead.
His hard night hit him too hard,
Or, perhaps, he'd had enough

Of stumbling, drunken,
Through the dance-floor's
Flashing
Thunder, sniffing
Poppers, popping
Pills, perusing
All the other
Unpursue-ables.

Because he was nineteen
And almost pretty
In his pale, lean, half-
Crazed way, because
His brittle little laugh
Cracked loudest, keeping questions
All at bay, because
because
He gave away,
On darker days,
What some would trade
For pay, because
He drew a lucid music
From raw rudeness
And real wisdom from
One-liners, and knew
Where
And how
And when to
Wear
Those
Clothes,

Because he paid the cost of chaos
And kept going,
We assumed
He really knew
What he was doing;
We assumed

Jack Veasey

He'd just passed out
And not passed
On (left on the landing
Covered roughly with
A blanket, safe
Since we had lugged him
Home.) He *had* been
Cold, but being cold
Was Eddie's way.

We had been through this
With him
A hundred times—

And, when the midday came,
He'd always waken, white
As bone, blood-
Shot, and groan
From his sick stomach
And hurt head.

This time, there were two differences:
He didn't wake,
And worse,
We couldn't blame him (though
We also couldn't bear to blame
Ourselves)

Because
He wore the brash mask
Of a bad boy, got it up
And gave good head, no matter
What stuff spiked his mind,
Because
Of all the blinding things he did
And all the stinging little things
He said, we thought
He knew what he was doing,
Knew the way back
And would wake
As on so many other whacked-out mornings
When the leaky popper in his pocket
Filled the room with fumes
And we woke,
Choking.

Jack Veasey

But Eddie's dead,
And chemicals can't cure him
Of this final crashing
Come-down.

I forget things
When my battered brain's
Been sealed off
From the hungry world
I live in, colored
By a drugged abundance,

But I remember
Eddie, slouched
In shadow, staring
Past the strobe-struck
Dancers, staring
Far beyond the bar-room
That became his universe
Of youth and beauty
By way of a flashing light;
Looking farther off
Than in his normal
Hardened pose, as if
His place were then
Another
Altogether.
I remember catching glimpses
Of the look he always wore
In those rare moments, when
His thick defenses dropped
Because he really thought
Nobody else was looking.
His look

Looked like a look
I think I sometimes wear
Myself, when
I am trying, staring
Silently and straining, dazed
But trying nonetheless,
When I am trying
To imagine
Happiness.

What he was thinking

In such moments, no one asked,
And now it's anybody's guess
As to who that lost boy was
Or what he thought, or
What he felt, or even
Wanted.
Sometimes,
In a single flash
Of strobe
That frames the dance-floor
Like a snapshot,
I could swear
I see his face,
And the face I see
Is wearing that same look
Of vacant eyes
And naked need—

But Eddie looked so much
Like many people,
And the face
Is a mistake.

Jack Veasey

WHEN I REINCARNATE

I want to come back as a biker chick,
Get passed around (at first) from guy to guy
Like a cheap bottle
That tastes better
Than it should. Let me
Get gang banged
On the green felt of
The pool table,
And leave a deep impression
Of my legendary ass. Let me
Rock the clubhouse
So they'll all want
One more taste,
Although they never
Dreamed they would. Let me
Provide the inspiration
For knife fights
Between the Bros,
For tattoos
That immortalize me—
Till that fatal accident
Or liver failure.

I want to be the subject of
A jukebox song, one
Guys will wait in line to play.
Let me be
That mistake
That breaks up
The bland marriages
At last, and
Let me be long gone
When hubby turns around.
Let me leave behind
The mark, the sting, the scent
That sticks
Forever. Let me be like
The road
That left them
Restless.

GRIN AND BEAR

We argued in your truck
Out on the road.
I can't remember
The subject, only
A welcome interruption:
As you flashed
Your hot blue eyes at me,
A black bear came
Scampering out of the woods
Into our path, oblivious
To us as you, the driver,
Were to him. I lay my hand
Gently on your thigh. "Look,"
I said, in a quieter voice
Than either of us had been using.

You did. You saw.
As if feeling
Your eyes on him,
The bear looked up at us.
Startled, he jumped straight up
Into midair, like some old
Cartoon character—all four paws
Left the ground at the same time.
He turned and scampered
Back into the woods—
And that's
The only verb for it;
Delicately, like a romping lamb.

We both
Forgot our argument. We'd both known
That this area had bears, but neither of us
Had seen one before.
We shared a grin, and drove on
In delighted silence.
I left my hand
Where it was.

Jack Veasey

THE HUSTLER

A street hustler leans
On a grated storefront,
Letting the lights
Of cars passing
Illumine his torso.

T-shirt
Tight with one rip
Under one armpit, cotton white
Against tan flesh, stretching
When he half turns
To follow eyes
That take note of him.

Drivers in a slow line
Circle the block like sharks.
Headlights make his shadow large.
His mind is
    Hidden.
How much
will the money pay for,
how much more
if the spirit should move him?
Does he consider this
War, and would the cost
Of a perceived loss set him off?

What is a man
To this fast-aging boy?
What's his measure
In a mirror?
Waves of heat
Distort his face.
His signal
    Wavers,
Crackling
Like a sudden fire.

JEFF WALT

A Daddy By Midnight

JEFF WALT's poems have appeared in journals such as *Alligator Juniper, Poetry International, New Millennium Writings, Harpur Palate*, and *The Cream City Review*. Recent anthologies include *Gay City: Vol. 3–RePulped* (Gay City Anthologies, 2010) and *TOUCHING: Poems of Love, Longing, and Desire* (Fearless Books, 2011). His chapbook, *Soot*, was co-winner of the 2009 Keystone Chapbook Prize and published in 2010 by Seven Kitchens Press.

www.jeffwalt.com

Jeff Walt

COMING TOGETHER

Drenched in summer sweat, I beg,
Wait, don't come yet.
The candle burns to its wick.
The heat and humidity match
the intensity of our want:
fire inside and out.
Your face contorts with pleasure—
near the end, spent, but still I beg, *Wait for me,*
as I rush to catch up. My greedy tongue
travels your body like the child I was
running among the dunes of the Cape—
mysterious, wild, free.
I wonder how people beyond these walls
can sleep knowing the pleasure
their bodies contain as you scream,
Yes! – More! – Harder! – Faster! – God!
until the moment—like two runners
neck and neck at the end of their race—
I demand *Now!* and we cross
the finish line as one, come together,
trembling, out of breath.
The wick flickers to its end
and the room goes completely black.
I say *I love you*, but already
you are asleep, your wet back turned
to me, so I roll to the opposite side
of the bed, find comfort in the cool
wall as I trace old, dried veins of paint
with my thumb. I do not need
to be next to you to know you love me—
it is in the numb joy of my tongue,
the ache of my hip, the pulse beneath
my nipples that recalls your lips.

Jeff Walt

EVENING VOICES

Mothers call the names
of their children
into the late evening.
Their hard voices echo
in the streets.
We sit on the edge
of the bed after sex,
in the silence
within the silence.
Happy words rush to my lips
but turn back swiftly.
I wish for the past, the days
we lived together and loved.
Remember hours spent wading
in the calm lake? The day you read
forever in my palm? You say
nothing exists beyond our
own breathing in this room,
but I know there is a chest of drawers,
a bureau and lamp, comfort
in the stillness cooled
by dusk's final breaths.
We are startled to hear your name
drift through the window,
some woman calling her son home
for dinner. Your body reacts:
the head lifts, the neck stretches
like that of some frightened bird.
Should you go to her—as if
the voice were your own mother shouting
through years of grief? Quickly
you pull me back onto the dirty sheets,
deep into the rage
of your lips and hands and tongue.

Jeff Walt

OROGENY

All day ice breaks from the eaves
in wet, geometric cones—

the plastic stapled to the window panes slaps
heavy breaths of spring against the glass

as the world leans and tilts, shifts
her hips, lifts hills into mountains,

shakes to the song that wakes fossils
from their pre-historic, shale sleep.

Children bake cold mud-pies in the driveway.
They don't know the danger of being

inside a child's body.   A lone robin
splashes in the thawing front yard bath.

The screen door humps its latch and now
a black dog stares at me from the street.

I am scared. I think the thing is telekinetic
or my father reincarnated.

The kids throw stones and the beast runs
into bushes of burdocks.

They don't know their bikes will rust,
the spokes will bend. Houses can burn.

How the baby in last week's news
was discovered in a dumpster

but still breathing; the way a lamp can slant
a face into the constant, still-weeping hum of regret;

how, even now, the earth's crust smacks upward,
restless in its bed like a sleeping tyrannosaurus.

Unaware of the orogeny beneath, they go on
playing children's games.   Someone could

Jeff Walt

tell them words they've never heard—
touch them into definition,

so that all they might ever notice in early spring
is *not* games and *not* playmates,

but the way ice can break all day
from the eaves in wet, geometric cones.

Jeff Walt

POSTCARDS MY BROTHER USED TO SEND

I found the poetry, postcards, and photos
my brother sent me,
buried in a shoebox beneath the calm,
yellow chill of antiquity.

The skyscrapers and boardwalks
he called home rise to view
in my palm—torn and wrinkled
panoramic sights of city streets:

Castro, Commercial, Bleecker, Duval—
"Full," he wrote, "yet so empty."
I shuffle his happiness
in my hands: still-lifes

of his errant ways scattered before me
like playing cards. I see him in each.
His boyish face, neon-drenched,
cities where—I've heard—

men dance on pillars
in pink light, tight underwear,
laser beams pulsing
into chiseled torsos.

His poetry confused me: childhood,
masturbation, men together in bed.
Now his life is a blur on my carpet:
"Sis, you must come to New Orleans—

you'd love the French Quarter!"
I live an ordinary life here in Milford, Iowa
and my children will grow up
never knowing their lost uncle, going

slowly as I scrub the drawers of my hutch:
a complete resurrection and burial at once
for the boy whose peregrinations
became family. The last postcard

from Boston, barely legible, inscribed:
"It was the only life I had."—melodramatic,
a quote from a poem. The wake is tomorrow,
someplace Northeast, his remains blown

on winter snow, freezing until spring
when he'll grow into daffodils and azaleas,
second life, *true* beauty, reaching toward
the sun in daylight and the moon, safe moon.

LIKE GRETEL

I wanted to be the first
to go. Not the strong one
left behind squinting
away winter light,
scattering ashes blessed
with prayers I do not understand—
handfuls of you
on the wet snow. And me,
like Gretel looking back
at the trail of ash, my tracks
following me deeper
into the dark wood.

Jeff Walt

SIZE

My buddy Jim wants a bigger penis,
he tells me, sitting outside *la Petite Patisserie*
where we sip café au laits on a Commercial Street, stare

longingly at 20 inch biceps, thick thighs
zipped inside tight Levi's; watch shirtless
skateborders with rippled abs float past

like the dreams of bodies we wish we had.
I sip from a huge mug—one minute
feeling insignificant and small like the fly

feeding off my dry fiber muffin, and in the next, large
and important as the 32 oz. Slushie the chubby kid
crossing the street is struggling to keep hold of.

My friend slowly stirs his Earl Grey, tells me
he wants to exchange his body, simply toss it
easily as an unwanted coat onto a store counter.

How small is it?
He holds up three fingers, explains fat sucked
from the gut can be injected under the skin.

He keeps asking if he should
have the operation. How can I advise
when I stand in front of a mirror

and snip white hairs each morning
before work, voraciously rub vanishing cream
on age spots that blotch my skin, keep secret

the bifocals that slide down my nose
when I read? *Waiter, Sir!*
—I need to yell—*Please bring me an éclair!*

Make it the sweetest,
biggest, fattest
one you've got.

WATCHING

No matter what man she was fucking, my mother
screamed loud as a woman trapped inside
a burning house. I'd jump

from puzzles, maps & plots
to her bedroom door
where I watched

cigarettes burn to their ends
in an ashtray full of butts, the men
preaching into her—

the gimp plumber, a blond pawning Electrolux
door-to-door, our landlord:
slick twines

of flesh, sheets, & sweat.
I'd wait for the roof of their lust to cave—
those last, seemingly

painful seconds before
the fire doused. Quiet afterward:
his hands twisting her

long, wet hair up in a slick braid
as she licked his stomach clean, or
her ear pressed to the heat

of his chest, listening
to the heart's senseless mumble. Then the woman
I watched fall

shit-faced from strange cars
& crawl across the lawn, might begin singing
passionately.

Sometimes
she would cry, the back of one hand lightly
rubbing the man's stubble...

sometimes
both palms open above the warmth

of his rising & falling chest. Once

on her knees beside the bed, like a lady
searching the charred debris
of a torched house

to find one thing
she could make
beautiful again.

Jeff Walt

A COMMON LIFE

> *When you return to something you love,*
> *it's already beyond repair.*
> *You wear it broken.*
>   —James L. White

I loved her once, loved
being smothered by her touch, her soft voice
calling me to bed. The men that loved her
are gone, too.

I've never watched anyone die
before, never waited for angels to unleash
their singing, unable to pray for hope
or life; for my mother's suffering.

She twists in misery, reaches
through years of regret, a common life
at its end, presses her frail hand in mine,
begs forgiveness for a life lived wrong.

Some days it seems poetry can be woven
from anything at all: sex, dusk opening
its wings above me, or a mother
on her deathbed trying to say *I love you*

for the first time. I read Cavafy to comfort us:
I do not dare whisper / what I wish to tell you: /
that to live without you / Is an unbearable penalty for me....
What kind of bullshit is that? she asks, laughs,

turns from me to her oxygen tank.
She says she's ready to go, ready
for whatever comes next.
I sit in a rocker beside her bed,

begin a slow, contemplative rhythm,
discover comfort in the wild dance she spun in bars,
how she held me in her arms above the lights
of a dusty jukebox, let me pick the songs,

promised me a daddy by midnight.

DESMOND KON ZHICHENG-MINGDÉ

This Electric Shine

DESMOND KON ZHICHENG-MINGDÉ has edited more than ten books and co-produced three audio books, several pro bono for nonprofit organizations. A former journalist, Desmond has traveled to Australia, France, Hong Kong and Spain for his stories and authored the limited edition Top Ten TCS Stars for Caldecott Publishing. Trained in publishing at Stanford, with a theology masters (world religions) from Harvard and fine arts masters (creative writing) from Notre Dame, he is the recipient of the Tom Howard High Distinction Award, Tupelo Press Poetry Project Honorable Mention, Hiew Siew Nam Academic Award, and Singapore Internationale Grant. An interdisciplinary artist, he also works in clay, his commemorative pieces housed in museums and private collections in India, the Netherlands, the UK and the US.

ARS POETICA BY TURNS

> *In sorrow, you must softer methods keep;*
> *And to excite our tears, your self must weep:*
> *Those noisy words with which ill Plays abound,*
> *Come not from hearts that are in sadness drown'd.*
> —Nicolas Boileau-Despréaux, L'Art poétique

I am particular about instant rapture
and how we elevate ourselves
to a higher civilization, like a tango.

I am swinging skirts; they arc multifarious
like rhizomes and Guattari becomes
my lover. I love the handsomeness of lost bearings

a man's speech to make random my past
our past. We are growing mushrooms
and onions and ginger. He likes ginger in his tea;

ginger makes his tea tart like shrapnel
hitting every mark. What will he mark next
a walking target, friend conversing over lunch?

But people mark him for the mess
the mess that only precipitates
all our illusions, all our foamy hypocrisy.

He even sweeps the clouds aside
like danger and resistance and constraint.
He even shares his plate and palate, happy painters.

He sheds his dance shoes and walks down three flights
sprints up two, and waits for more commands, more calls
to narrate how this must be done

how that must be done, how all of us are undone.
We are all our undoing, the rhizome
paints for us through its trajectory.

We are all our ultimates like a voice.
You try to draw bee-lines like sunshine
but our light does not travel in straight lines.

No, we travel like bumbling bees and fingers down frets
even if all it is is noise that we make, even if
all there ever was was ever that, my and your noise.

Desmond Kon Zhicheng-Mingdé

EUDAEMONISM IN A SENRYU NOVEL

that one's new fiction
remains on the shore, its sand
a clean slate, of shale

and a lithosphere
so together, angels buck
unsaddled riders

that muscles and arch
untether wings, village tale
turned big history

turned siltstone, hammer
brought to its edge, a chisel
to bear its own weight

NOMINALISM IS A LIQUID KUHI

solomonic column, white
scraped clean of spirals

here lies a similar name
safe, lamp-lit passage

maybe tomorrow, a shine

as a flute flourished
flushed garlands atop, around
us wet down, barley sugar

too extravagant with hope?
frugal enough with old dreams?

preserved, these dreams flower white

as sitting exhorts us, still
as a liturgy cooing
its soliloquy

new and different
a silent weeping, whisper
to recover this—

an ice-sheet soul, white
flash, bright glacial creak

AS WITH A SENRYU'S POOLING TEARS

old town draped in flags
its atrium decked with horse carts
green cabs in tow

the groom in a kilt—

displace the redder letter
to open the doors

loud jingle of white
japanese pieris snowing—
fall of southern catalpa

behind handsewn ornaments
strewn, train of chiffon

briskly lit, clapping
sublunary and nearing—

dull glow, this electric shine

SOCIAL REALISM IS A TABLE NAPKIN OF HAIKU

slip on pinewood squares
feldspar, talc, red clay, plaster—
chrome stains on loveseat

la vie en rose, this—
where's the orange-eyed sparrow?
stage life, force, beeswax

long grain like moonstone
poured into brown porcelain—
lank, terraced, lowlands

four ideas installed—
for more conceptual art, this
moment like whale song

Desmond Kon Zhicheng-Mingdé

A SENRYU BESIDE THE CYLINDERS

armchair upholstered
oak chair and four broken legs
a stool on its side

blue stars on gypsum
lamp-lit room, feathers, something
metaphysical

like duchamp, brothers
in a double bind, not so
monomoraic

not matter of fact
or so easy a story
its ghosts human shapes

A FADED POSTCARD IS A TANKA DAYDREAM

but of the firewalker
of his frame, a rush of flame

look at both faces, closed eyes

this, what you were born into
to grasp, that expectation
a forward hesitation—

to love only once
to endure, outlast these worlds
a lowing, literal love

not the bitter deathsong ends
not the judging eyes

a milk bath before
fresh plate of malai kofta

look at the firewalker—

dusted feet and flake, embers
as windblown, the water oak
next to the winged spindle tree

AS WITH RECITATION AND THE LOSS OF A KUHI

this thieving of love
tightrope against what it means—
to visit the past

who is good; who wrong?
which brittle, yellowing build?

of old, bluing tarpaulin?

uniform as points, squares, lined
instincts and numbers primed too

quiet eyes like dark opal
their squircle an open seat
under chestnut shade

as with basho on his mat

there he lays, small, crouched
under a low-lying cave
its long, empty lake

praetoria of ruins gone

fingers curled into his palm
unfurling, unclenched—

tired hope for newer days

SOLARISM IS A LEANING OF SENRYU

gap between chance and premise
its inches three steps too wide

not the nonetheless or please
not forever of nods
or a walk to corner street

this sun eclipsing itself

naked, your body a sheen
backlit, the thrust stage ornate

no aprons on the sidewalk
as with the sun and their eyes

who will bury the adage?

velvet mood to dull
senses as muddy, half moon
no walls and stopped time

Desmond Kon Zhicheng-Mingdé

AS WITH ATOMISM A PEARLESCENT SENRYU

what is knowable
in the here and now and world
of visible things?

what psychology
in the mix, squares suspended
like this doubt, staying

cyclorama, white
repainted over with red dye
a deep, loveless hue

the monad stilling
like a stray flower landing—
rock garden quiet

RHETORIC IS A HAIKU IN HIGH RELIEF

a noonday eclipse
no matter what happens
we meet, bistre junction

no matter rain or moonshine
we exchange stories—

no matter, the path will stay
the road till then

between thumb and finger
a blessing—relic
from the chapel

its shrine shimmering
vast blanket light

then night again and an owl

hope in the new days
we approach the green vista
ceil words in backpack

GAVIN GEOFFREY DILLARD

A Poem for Ian Young

IAN YOUNG co-founded the first Canadian gay liberation group in 1969 and created the groundbreaking gay literary press, Catalyst, the following year. In 1973, he edited *The Male Muse*, an early, daring, and important anthology of gay poets which was followed in 1983 by *The Son of the Male Muse: New Gay Poetry*. His decades-long friendship with GAVIN GEOFFREY DILLARD has been chronicled in numerous poems written by both men over the years. Here, Gavin continues the tradition.

Gavin Geoffrey Dillard on Ian Young

ODE TO IAN: A SCARBOROUGH LAD

I met Master Ian in a bleak apartment on the corner of St Marks and 2nd Avenue—the Bowery. A dark-bearded exotic, he had a cleft lip, Britannic accent, and uncut willie. He devoured books the way other folk thumb magazines; I was still in high school, an art student, fingers stained with the ink of nights wrestling with unruly Underwood typewriter ribbon. Stevie Wonder's *Fulfillingness* was our soundtrack.

It was the Dawn of Time, an icy winter of '73 or '74; Ian was publishing my first book of verse, as we hobnobbed with the Malangas, the Ginsbergs and Rorems. The apartment had a modicum of heat, but no hot water; we boiled our bath water in pots and mimicked the Italian woman upstairs who was going to slit her husband's throat (or her own). There was always a prostrate body on the front stoop to step over—we never checked for breath.

Now he lives in a Mongolian yurt on the frigid Canadian tundra, a Wulf is his constant companion. An ushanka, pink tutu and tights, mukluks the color of spilled wine; the fatuousness of poetry has been superseded by plantings, stacks of wood and dried bundles of herbs, tho books are still rallied in wheel barrow and crates. Ian is the foremost queer herstorian in the world.

The gods challenge such men with the leaden curse of reason, then applaud when the craziness sets in. I went on to conquer the world; Ian remained, calmly, Master of the Universe. Decades later the bard writes a blurb for the cover of my twelfth volume, *Nocturnal Omissions*. The blatherings of the New York literary élite no longer hold sway, in our respective abbeys, nor indeed relevance; witches and Time Lords tend to their berries and brambles.

SETH RUGGLES HILER

My Black-Haired Adonis

SETH RUGGLES HILER, cover artist for this issue of *Assaracus*, creates and records connections to people and places through painting and drawing. He received a BFA in painting from Syracuse University in 2002 and an MFA from the New York Academy of Art in 2005. He now maintains a studio in Boonton, New Jersey, and is an adjunct professor at Bard High School Early College in Newark, New Jersey. Seth's work is exhibited in solo and group exhibitions at galleries and institutions throughout the Northeast and in Ontario, Canada, including the Morris Museum in New Jersey, New York City's Salmagundi Club and Syracuse University. In 2010, the Monmouth Museum of Art featured his work in the solo exhibition "New Jersey Emerging Artists Series: Seth Ruggles Hiler—Portraits." The premiere of "Ash Unravel," a dance and drawing collaboration with dancer-choreographer Michael Caldwell, was presented in Toronto in August of 2011 at the Dance Made in Canada Festival. Guerilla Galleries in Newark, New Jersey, presented "CROPPED, An Intimate View," a solo show of large graphite portraits in September 2011.

www.sethruggleshiler.com

SUBMIT TO ASSARACUS

The mission of Sibling Rivalry Press is to develop, publish, and promote outlaw artistic talent—those projects which inspire people to read, challenge, and ponder the complexities of life in dark rooms, under blankets by cell-phone illumination, in the backseats of cars, and on spring-day park benches next to people reading Kirby Congdon. We encourage submissions to *Assaracus* by gay male poets of any age, regardless of background, education, or level of publication experience. Submissions are accepted during the months of January, May, and September. For more information, visit us online.

SUBSCRIBE TO ASSARACUS

Readers can subscribe to receive a year of *Assaracus*. The subscription price is $50.00 for U.S. readers and $80.00 for international readers (including shipping), which buys you four book-length (120+ pages), perfect-bound issues of our grand stage for gay contemporary poetry. Subscriptions are available through our website.

NEW FROM SIBLING RIVALRY PRESS

He Do the Gay Man in Different Voices by Stephen Scott Mills: Unable to accept complacency in suburban life, Mills transports himself to dank prison cells, international executions, and the minds of murderers that unravel through the kinky underbelly of America. He comes full-circle back to the bedroom of a young, gay couple whose everyday lives surprise us in a flawed and fascinating world. *He Do the Gay Man in Different Voices* channels the hushed tones, loving whispers, and lusty moans of a generation deluged in an unflinching, unending media assault that brings the best and worst of us to an exciting, terrifying proximity.

"If you're someone who's ever gone home with a stranger, after reading *He Do the Gay Man in Different Voices*, you'll feel lucky to be alive: unraped, unmurdered, uneaten."

—Jeremy Halinen, author of *What Other Choice*

www.siblingrivalrypress.com

CPSIA information can be obtained at www.ICGtesting.com
Printed in the USA
LVOW07s0742140514

385621LV00004BA/423/P